Victorian clothes

Fiona Reynoldson

This book is about the clothes worn by a particular Victorian family, their servants and the people who visited them. The sorts of clothes people wore tell us a lot about what life was like in Victorian times.

If you are using the book to find out particular facts about Victorian clothes, you do not have to read it all. Look at the **contents** (below) or the **index** (at the back) to find the best pages to help you. Then just read as much as you need to read.

The basic facts are given in big print, and more detailed information is in smaller print.

Contents

1 Introduction

In Victorian times, there were all sorts of people living in Britain. There were rich and poor people. There were women, men and children. There were servants, shopkeepers, engineers, factory workers, dustmen, office workers, and farm workers. There were townspeople and country people.

Rich people often wore fashionable clothes made of silk, fine wool, velvet, and furs. Ordinary people wore more practical clothes made of hard-wearing wool or cotton.

This book is about the clothes worn by business people in late Victorian times. It also describes the clothes that their servants wore, and the clothes of the people who called at their houses. The book uses the Gray family as an example of a business family.

 This painting of a London street was made in 1888.

2 The Gray family in 1882

The man in the photograph is Frank Barton Gray.
He was a baker in Shanklin, Isle of Wight.
His wife, Kate, is the woman sitting down with
the baby on her knee.

All the members of the family are dressed in their best clothes for the photograph.

In Victorian times, families dressed in their best clothes and sat very still for a photograph to be taken. It could take as long as a whole minute for a photograph to be taken in the 1880s.

Frank Barton Gray was a baker in the small seaside town of Shanklin. He is sitting down in the photograph, with his son Frederick in front of him.

Frank Barton Gray was 35 years old when the photograph was taken, and his bakery business was beginning to do well.

His mother was poor, but his father was probably Barnabas Barton, a rich man in the town. Possibly Frank got the money to train as a baker and to start a business from his father. Nobody knows for sure.

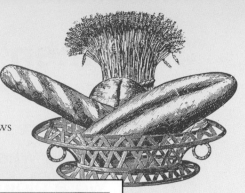

⬆ Frank Barton Gray is sitting down. His wife, Kate, is sitting holding the baby and the woman standing up is perhaps her sister.

Frank died soon after the photograph was taken. His wife took over the bakery business, and she ran it until her two sons were grown up. The girls in the photograph are Minnie (in the front), Elsie Kate, and baby Jessie. You can see that the baby moved while the photograph was being taken.

They all wore their best clothes. The girls have their hair done in ringlets. Kate's long hair is pulled back into a low bun at her neck while the other woman has a fashionable hair style. It is frizzed at the front and pulled into a bun at the back of the neck.

3 Women's clothes

Rich women wore very beautiful dresses made of silk. Women who worked at home or in a business wore plain dark dresses made of wool or cotton. Both rich and working women wore corsets all the time.

A woman wearing her best dress for going to visit friends.

A rich woman had many servants, and because she did not have to work hard, she could wear beautiful silk dresses.

A business woman like Kate Gray had three servants to help her with the house and with her children. Even so, she was very busy running the home and business. She usually wore dark dresses made of soft wool, so that she could both look smart and be warm. Like nearly all women of her time, Kate wore corsets to keep her in shape.

Kate Gray.

In Victorian times there was no nylon or polyester. There were many different fabrics made from wool, silk, and cotton. 'Cashmere' was fine wool taken from Kashmir goats and then woven in a certain way.

Wool was woven with cotton and silk to make different sorts of material such as 'Valencia' or 'Toilinette'.

Silk was woven with zig-zags and called 'Florentine', or woven thickly and called 'grosgrain'. If silk was woven and cut in a special way, it was called 'velvet'.

Rich women wore dresses made of silk or of silk mixtures. The dresses had frills, bows, and big sleeves. Working women like Kate Gray wore practical everyday dresses made of serge (wool), or of merino, which was a thin woollen cloth made from the wool of merino sheep.

Skirts were held out by petticoats and sometimes by a wire frame called a 'crinoline'. The dresses fitted tightly, so women wore corsets to give them the right shape for the dress and to support their muscles. Many people believed that tight corsets supported women's stomach muscles.

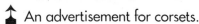
⬆ An advertisement for corsets.

4 Clothes for children and nannies

All children wore lots of clothes to keep them warm.

Boys wore jackets and trousers for every day.
Girls wore dresses with big white aprons over them.
Women or girls called nannies looked after the children.

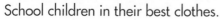 School children in their best clothes.

▲ Children always had to wear hats, even at the seaside.

There was no central heating in houses in those days, so children wore plenty of clothes to keep them warm.

When they were little, both boys and girls like the Gray children wore dresses and petticoats. Boys started to wear woollen trousers and jackets before they went to school. Girls wore dark dresses and white starched aprons or pinafores over their dresses. Both boys and girls wore hats when they went out.

The Gray family employed a young servant called a 'nanny'. Her job was to look after the children. She took them for walks down to the seashore and out into the country. She also had to be good at sewing and mending their clothes.

This was written in the *English Woman's Domestic Magazine*, in 1880: "A sailor hat in brown straw, trimmed with black ribbon with bow ends, is suitable for little boys six to seven years of age."

Skirts and petticoats made of wool and flannel kept small children warm.
Once they went to school, boys wore tweed suits which felt very scratchy.
They wore shirts with stiff, starched collars, and floppy ties.

Girls wore woollen or cotton dresses covered by big white aprons or pinafores
to keep the dresses clean.

Washing was a big job every week in every household, because there were no
washing machines. Often a washerwoman came in for the day to help the maid,
and together they boiled up water and scrubbed clothes on a wash-board.

The day after wash day was ironing day. All the white shirts, aprons, blouses,
caps and petticoats had to be ironed with flat-irons which were heated on the stove.
Many of the white clothes were starched to make them stiff, so that everyone
went out looking clean and smart.

In many families the nanny helped on
wash-day and she often did some of the mending
of the children's clothes.

Most of her time was spent with the young
children. She dressed them, got their meals, took
them out, played with them, bathed them,
and got them ready for bed.

◄◄ A boy in his best clothes.

11

5 What cooks and maids wore

The cook and the maids in a Victorian household, such as the Grays', often wore cotton dresses and white caps. The kitchen maid wore an old apron while she was working.

▲ A woman using a wooden tool called a dolly to do the washing.

The cook wore a plain dark cotton dress. She wore a white starched cap and a very large apron that reached to the floor.

The maid wore a plain cotton dress, or even a check gingham dress. In the mornings it was covered by an old apron while she was doing the cleaning. In the afternoon she changed her apron for a clean white one and a smart cap with ribbons hanging from it. In rich homes she might change from her working cotton dress into a black dress in the afternoon.

An advertisement from *The Times* newspaper in 1879.

A thorough Cook WANTED in a gentleman's family in the country. A kitchenmaid is kept. A steady respectable person required. Must be able to bake bread, cure hams and make good butter, as there is a small dairy. Address stating wages required, where and with whom she has worked and her age to Mrs. Warren, Ness House, Ipswich.

 A parlour maid wearing her best uniform to serve tea.

13

The cook rolled up the sleeves of her plain cotton dress when she was cooking, or sometimes she wore washable sleeve-covers to protect her good dress. Like nearly all women, she wore corsets and plenty of petticoats. She and the maid had woollen stockings and good leather lace up shoes.

The maid worked very hard. She lived in the house. She got up at 6 a.m. to clean out the fires and light them. Then she heated water and carried it upstairs in jugs, so that the family could wash. Then she helped the cook to get the breakfast, and afterwards she washed up. They both cleaned and swept and dusted the house.

When this was over, the maid changed her coarse old apron for a smart white one, so that she could serve tea and open the door to visitors. Sometimes she changed her dress as well. The maid had to serve the dinner and clear up afterwards so she was lucky to be in bed by 10.30 p.m. She might have a half-day off each week.

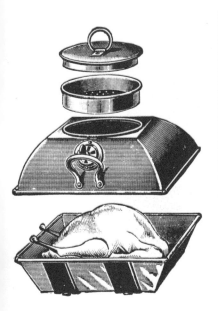

 A cook with one of the new gas stoves. Her apron fastens under her bustle.

6 Best clothes for women

Rich women had lots of best clothes made of silk and velvet. Even fairly rich women and girls often had one best dress of silk.

Poor women bought old clothes in markets, and servant girls were often given cast-off dresses by the women for whom they worked.

⬆ The rich women in this photograph are wearing silk dresses and lace trimmings.

By the middle of the 1880s the fashion was to have dresses with wide skirts, with a bustle at the back to hold the skirt out behind. All women wore hats and gloves when they went out, whether it was to go to church or to the music hall. Women's coats had to be made to go over the skirts and bustles, so cloaks and jackets were popular. Often coats were heavily decorated: they had beads and ribbons sewn on them.

A picture from a fashion magazine in the 1880s. ➤➤

Women's clothes were very complicated in the 1880s. A woman like Kate Gray wore a corset which made her look as if she had a very small waist. On top of this she wore a padded cage which made the dress stick out at the back. This was called a 'bustle'.

Even the woollen coats that women wore in cold weather were shaped to cover the bustle. The coats were trimmed with so many beads made of jet or lead that a winter coat might weigh as much as 10 kg. Women wore all sorts of hats, from old fashioned bonnets to sailor hats. Evening dresses were very frilly. They were made of silk and lace.

Fans were very popular. They were often enormous, and were made of feathers or lace or painted silk. A woman could fan herself to keep cool or she could hide a yawn behind her fan if she became very bored.

Only very rich women went to balls and huge parties, but many other women enjoyed a day out at the seaside, visited a music hall, attended parties at their friends' houses, or went to church.

Many women made their own dresses or had them made by local dressmakers. By the 1890s, skirts and blouses were becoming more popular than dresses.

Very poor women usually bought their clothes from second-hand markets or were given cast offs by the people for whom they worked.

⬆ There were lots of second-hand clothes stalls in city markets.

7 Best clothes for men

In late Victorian times, men such as Frank Gray wore jackets and trousers made of wool. They wore white shirts, and they wore different sorts of ties at the neck.

Men always wore hats when they went outside. They put on a hat to go to work, to go out for a walk, or to visit friends.

⬆ Inside an omnibus (which was later shortened to bus). Omnibus means 'for everyone'.

A family in 1890. All the men are wearing different jackets.

In late Victorian times, young men wore different styles of jackets and trousers. Older men often wore long dark jackets called 'frock-coats'. They also wore white shirts with high collars and bow ties. Men always wore hats when they went out. Rich men wore black silk top hats when they were dressed in their best clothes.

From about 1890, younger men wore different sorts of hats. Some of these were made of felt, which was cut and stretched into different shapes. There were bowlers, trilbys, wide-awake hats, and homburgs. In the summer, boaters made of straw were popular.

19

8 Callers at the house

All sorts of people called at houses to deliver things or to take them away.

The postman, the baker and the milkman called every day. The butcher and the fishmonger called once a week. The dustman, the coalman and the sweep called less often.
They all wore dark woollen clothes, hats on their heads, and aprons of some sort.

↑ A butcher's shop.

⬆ Men delivering coal. The coal was tipped directly into the cellar.

The baker and milkman called at houses like the Grays' each day with bread and milk. They dressed smartly and often wore aprons.

The butcher called once or twice a week depending on how much meat the household ate. He wore a blue and white striped apron, and a straw boater on his head.

The fishmonger wore a large apron which smelt strongly of fish, because he wiped his hands on it.

The dustman, the coalman and the sweep had very dirty jobs, so they wore old clothes covered by aprons made of sacking. The dustman and the coalman had soft hats with a flap at the back to protect their necks when they carried the heavy sacks.

21

9 What bakers wore

Many people bought bread from a baker who called at the house. The bakers got up very early to make the bread each day. They wore ordinary clothes covered with huge white aprons. The fresh bread was delivered to people's houses.

 The baker's boy has baskets full of bread to deliver to people's houses.

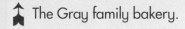 The Gray family bakery.

The Grays' bakery was a big building and was very hot because of the ovens. The bakers worked with their shirt sleeves rolled up as they kneaded the dough and put the loaves in the ovens.

They started work as early as 3 or 4 a.m., and soon looked white and dusty all over from the flour that they used. The bread was baked by 7 a.m.

The bakery boys took the baskets of bread and rolls to the carts, and went from house to house delivering the breakfast rolls.

A bakery in a small town had several delivery carts, and five or six horses to pull them. The boys were smartly dressed and often wore straw boaters on their heads.

10 Postmen's uniforms

Postmen called at every house. They wore a uniform of a blue coat and trousers, both trimmed with red. They had stiff hats with a peak in front.

↑ A postman on a penny-farthing bicycle.

From 1793 all postmen wore uniforms. At first they wore scarlet coats with brass buttons. The postman's number was printed on each button. They also wore tall shiny hats and dark trousers.

The scarlet coats quickly got dirty, so in 1861 the uniform was changed to a dark blue coat trimmed with scarlet, and dark blue trousers with a thin scarlet stripe down the leg. The tall hat was replaced by a more practical peaked cap.

Flora Thompson wrote a book called *Candleford Green* about her childhood in late Victorian times:

"From the village Post Office, letters were distributed by a male postman, and for more outlying houses and farms by two women letter-carriers."

A postman before 1861.

11 Clothes for sport

In late Victorian times, sport was becoming popular with more and more people. They wanted to play tennis, or to play cricket, or to go out on bicycles, so they needed clothes that were more comfortable.

⬆ A women's cricket match in about 1890.

⬆ Getting on a bicycle was often difficult.

Women as well as men were becoming more interested in sport. Archery, tennis, and cycling were all becoming popular, but it was difficult to run around or to cycle in long, heavy skirts or tight dresses. Gradually women began to wear looser dresses. This was thought to be very daring.

27

Archery was popular for women as well as for men from the 1860s. No special clothes were needed for this sport. When it came to cycling and tennis, people had to be able to run around. Men started to wear open necked shirts and long white trousers for tennis, but they wore their ordinary clothes for cycling.

At first women played tennis in their day dresses and hats. They moved slowly, and patted the ball back and forth across the net.

When they cycled, some women were more daring. They wore divided skirts, which made it much easier to get on and off their bicycles. This was important, because special bicycles without crossbars were not made for women until the 1890s.

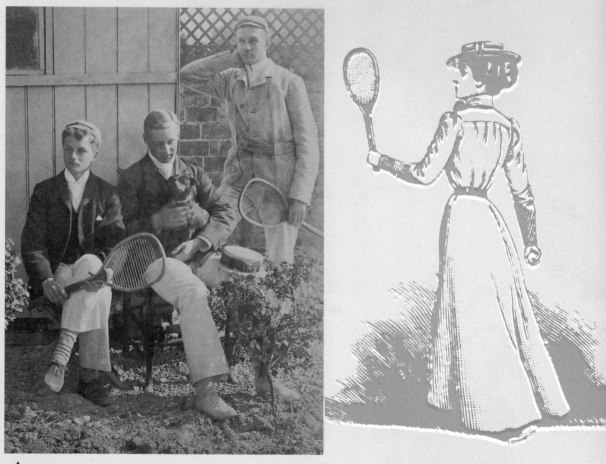

↑ Lawn tennis was becoming popular in the late 1800s.

By the 1880s there were other changes in women's lives too. Parliament said that a married woman could own her own things. Before this she did not even own the clothes that she wore. A married woman's right to own things gave her more freedom. The clothes women wore from late Victorian times onwards were lighter and freer. This showed the beginning of more freedom and independence for women.

12 Summary

There were so many people living in Victorian Britain, and they did so many different kinds of jobs that it is difficult to say exactly what clothes were worn by them all.

It is safe to say that people more or less followed the fashion of the time. How they followed it depended on how much money they had, how comfortable they liked to be, and what their jobs were. Bakers, butchers, policemen, and business women like Kate Gray had to wear clothes that were suited to what they did.

↑ The clothes worn by poor people.

◄◄ The clothes worn by rich people.

Some things about Victorian clothes do stand out. Women and children wore tight, heavy, restricting clothes, and this showed how they were expected to behave and to live. Men's clothes were much freer and more practical, and this showed the freer lives that they led. Clothes for everyone were stiffer and more formal than clothes are today, and this shows that the people lived their lives more stiffly and formally than we do nowadays.

Glossary

Apron　　　　An apron is a piece of cloth tied with strings round the waist. It protects the clothes from dust or water.

Boaters　　　Boaters are straw hats. They used to be worn by people going out in boats.

Bun　　　　　A bun of hair is a way of twisting long hair into a round shape.

Bustle　　　A bustle was a pad to make a skirt stick out at the back.

Cast off　　A cast off is something (often clothes) that a person does not want any more.

Corsets　　A corset is a tight fitting garment worn under the clothes to pull in the waist and flatten the stomach.

Cotton　　　Cotton comes from a vegetable plant. It can be woven to make thread which is then used to make clothes.

Crinoline　A crinoline was a large stiff petticoat made with steel wire. It was worn under a woman's skirt to make the skirt stick out all round.

Dough　　　Dough is flour and water mixed with yeast. When dough is baked it makes bread.

Flannel　　Flannel is a warm material made from wool.

Kneaded　　When something is kneaded it is pressed together. A baker presses and pummels dough before baking it.

Nylon　　　Nylon is a chemical which is used to make thread.

Pinafores　Pinafores were loose clothes like large aprons that covered dresses.

Polyester　Polyester is a chemical which is used to make fibres, plastics and yarn.

Restricting　Restricting means limiting. It often means stopping someone from doing something.

Silk　　　　Silk is a very light thread. It is flexible and elastic but also very strong.

Starched　Starch comes from plants. It is used to stiffen clothes, such as collars.

Wool　　　Wool is made from animal hair. It feels warm when you touch it.

Further information

The best way to find out more about Victorian clothes is to look for old postcard albums and old photos. There are many photos around in family albums.

You can visit local museums and picture galleries, local history groups and antique fairs. There are also costume museums such as the Costume Museum in Bath, Avon.

Further reading

Cocoa and Corsets by Michael Jubb, 1984, P.R.O.

How We Used To Live – Victorians Early and Late by David Evans, 1990, A. and C. Black and Yorkshire T.V.

Nineteenth Century English Costume by C & P Cunnington, 1959, Faber and Faber.

Index

a b c d e f g h i j k l m n o p q r s t u v w x y z
A B C D E F G H I J K L M N O P Q R S T U V W X Y Z